TO A *wonderful daughter*

LITTLE TIGER GIFT
An imprint of LITTLE TIGER PRESS
1 The Coda Centre, 189 Munster Road, London SW6 6AW
www.littletigerpress.com

First published in Great Britain 2013

Text by Josephine Collins, copyright © Little Tiger Press 2013
Illustrations copyright © Jill Latter 2013
Jill Latter has asserted her right to be identified as the illustrator
of this work under the Copyright, Designs and Patents Act, 1988

A CIP catalogue record for this book is available from the British Library

All rights reserved • ISBN 978-1-84895-524-0

Printed in China • LTP/1800/0505/1012

10 9 8 7 6 5 4 3 2 1

TO A *wonderful daughter*

LITTLE TIGER *Gift*

Daughter, you are...

so beautiful,

so clever,

so surprising,

so *wonderful!*

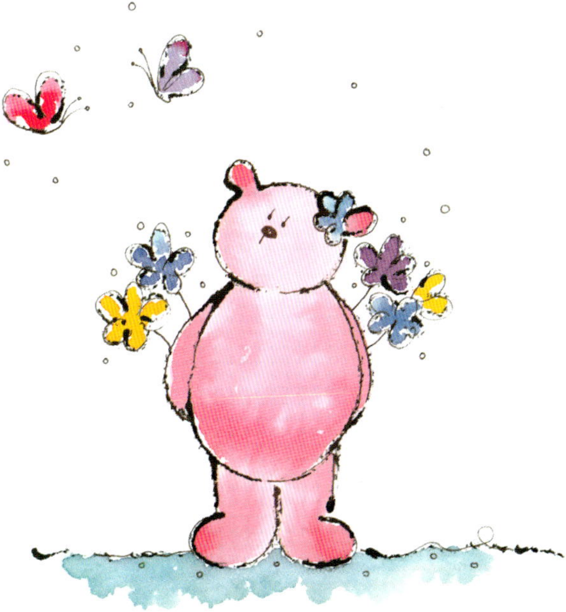

To have **YOU** as my daughter and my friend…

makes me the *happiest* person alive.

You only have to *smile*...

and my day is PERFECT!

I *remember*...

telling stories and laughing with you...

building dens and hiding with you...

dressing up and dancing with you!

Memories of *special* times.

It seems only yesterday that you were my little girl,

skipping along...

Now, LOVELY daughter, you are a beautiful woman,

dancing on her way!

From your FIRST smile,

your first step, your first word…

you have been — and always will be —

the *sunshine* in my world.

For ALL the fun and *messy* times,

the *magic* and the make-believe,

the laughter and *lovely* silliness...

thank you, my darling.

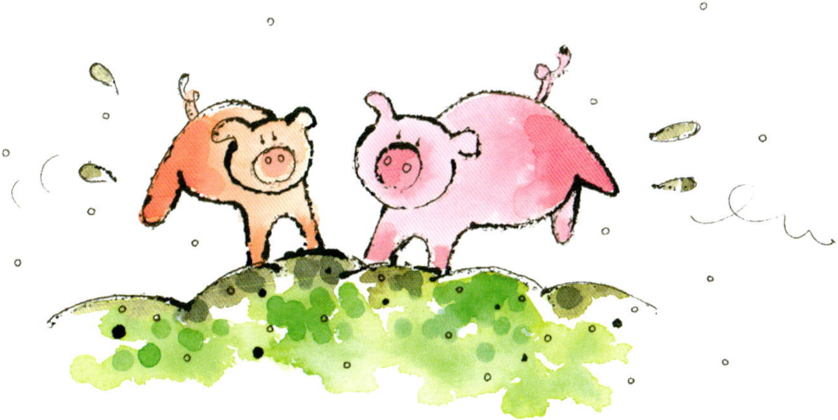

I love the *little* things you do!

If ever you're AFRAID,

I'll be there to *hold* your hand.

No matter how far away you are,

I *still* feel close to YOU.

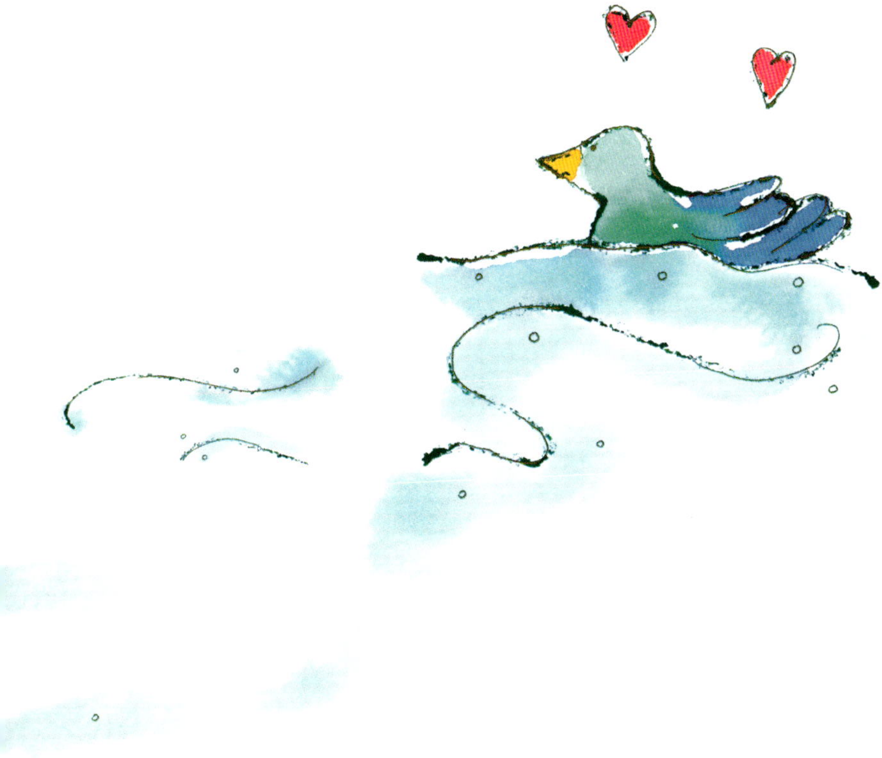

ALWAYS cheering you on…

   always on your side…

always there for a hug...

I'm always there for you,

my love.

I LOVE cooking you your *favourite* things!

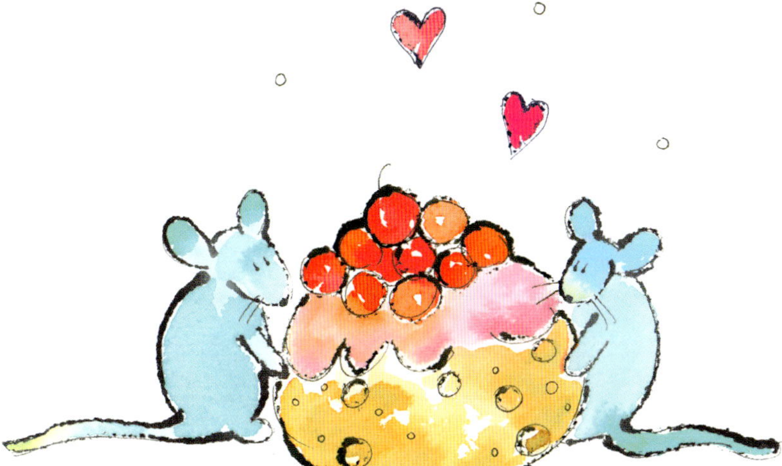

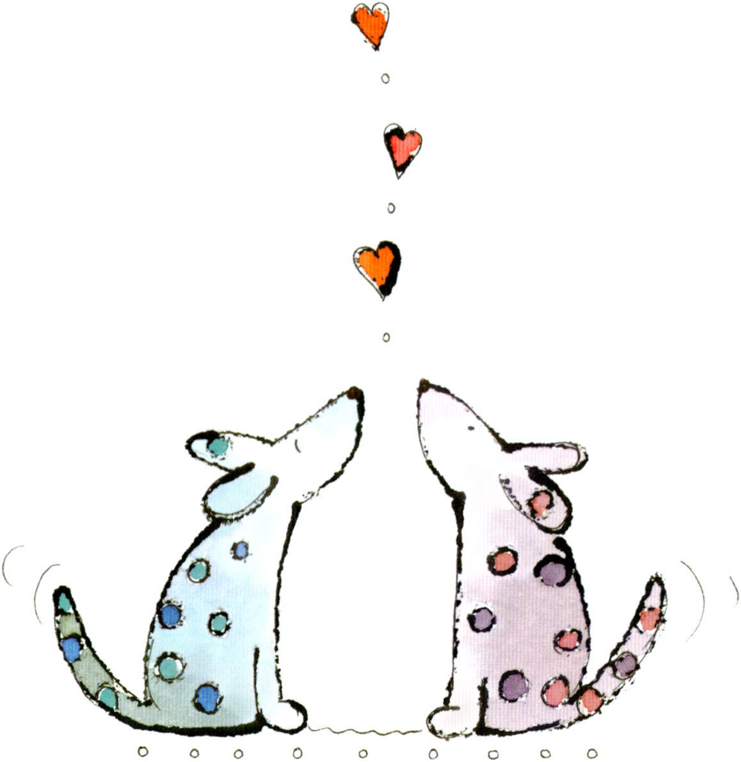

Laughing *together*...

chatting together...

HAPPY together!

Daughter, may you believe that **ANYTHING** is possible...

and may ALL your dreams come *true!*

You ALWAYS know how to *cheer* me up.

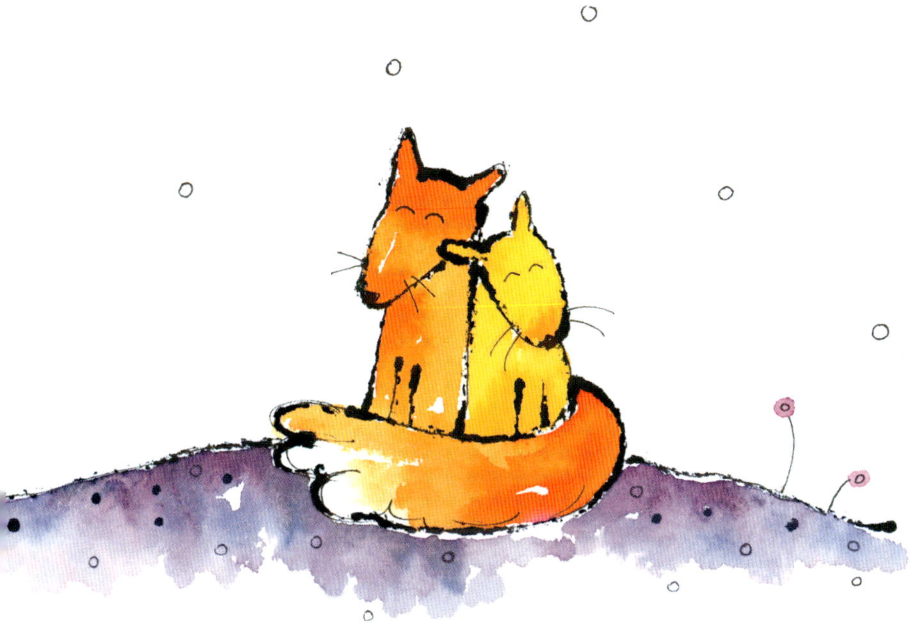

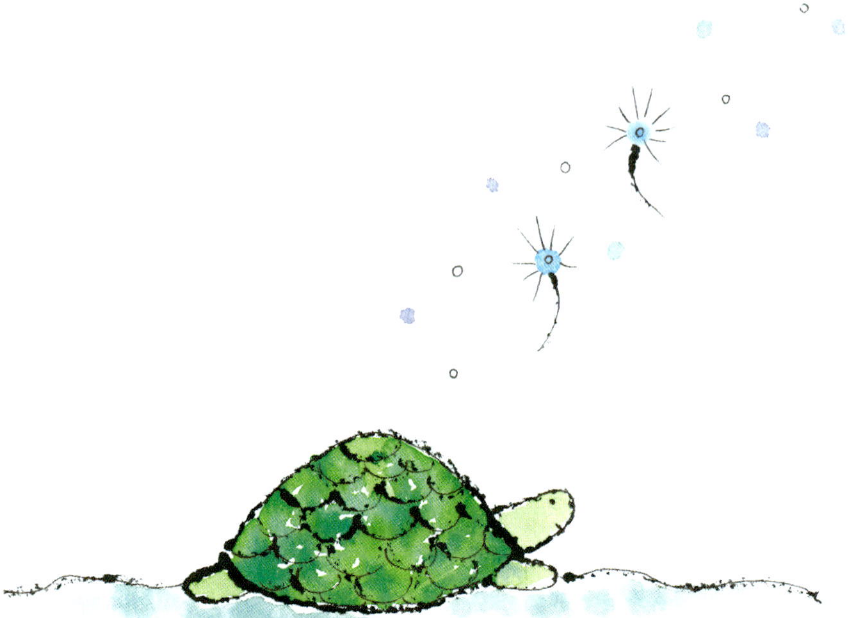

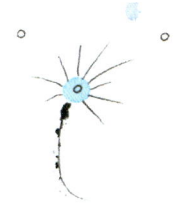

For all the messages and *wishes* you send me,

and all the KIND things you do...

thank you, lovely daughter!

Seeing you now,

so GROWN-UP,

so brave, so *kind*...

   makes me so proud.

Sometimes I just want to SHOUT OUT –

and tell the whole world how *brilliant* you are!

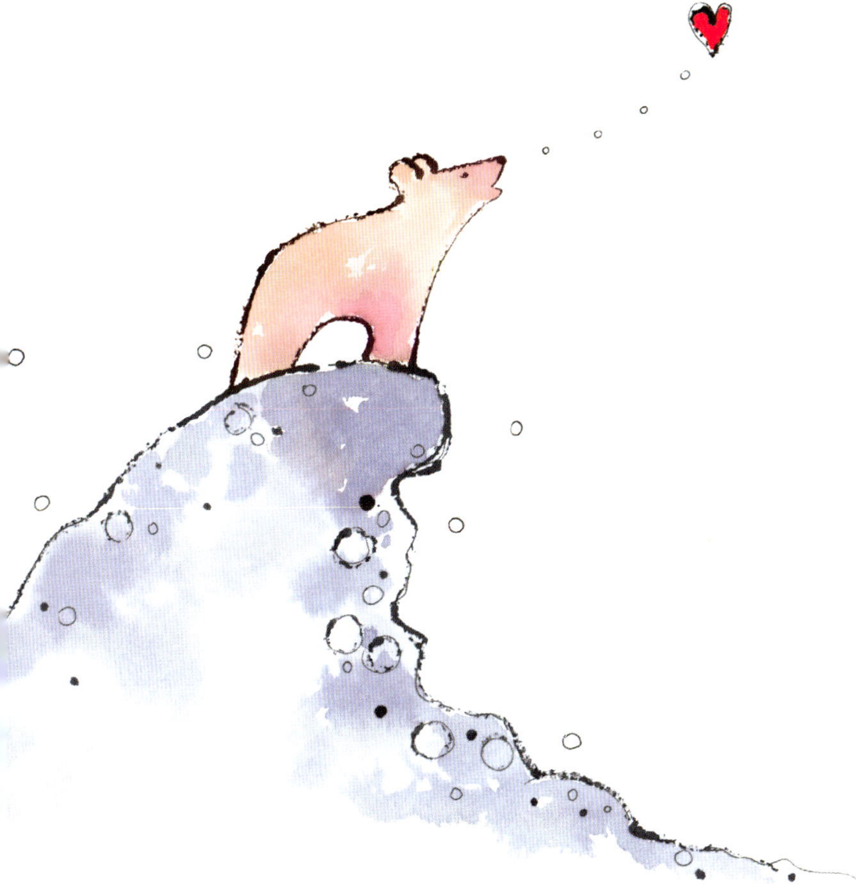

I hope you know how SPECIAL you are...

    how loved you are...

        wonderful,

           wonderful daughter!

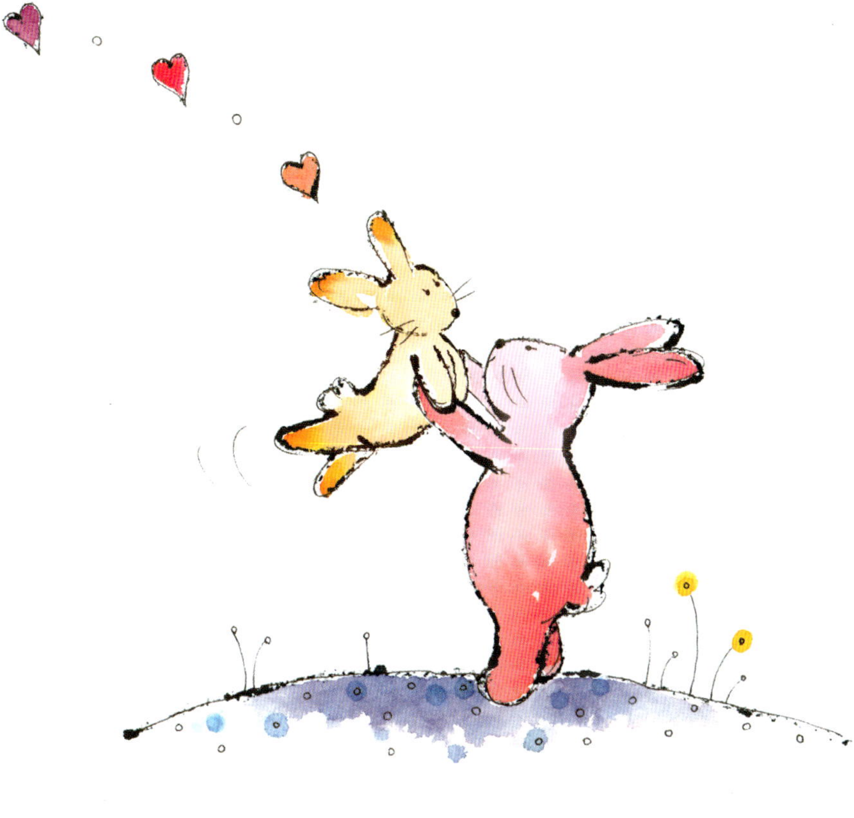